2022 ✓

2024: ✓

SO-AIA-848

Evolution of a Wine Drinker

Alicia Bien

Patriots Colony Library
Williamsburg, Virginia

Bien Entertainment, Inc.

EVOLUTION OF A WINE DRINKER
By Alicia Bien

Text Copyright © 2013 Alicia Bien
Cover photographs and
Illustrations Copyright © 2013 Wim Bien

All rights reserved.
No part of this book may be used or reproduced
in any manner whatsoever
without the written permission of Alicia Bien.

FIRST EDITION

ISBN: 978-0-9897000-1-0

For

Wim B.
With love, always

"When you come to a fork in the road, take it."

—Yogi Berra

"When you come to a bottle of wine in the road, drink it."

—Alicia Bien

TABLE OF CONTENTS

Dedication

Epigraph

ACKNOWLEDGEMENTS

ABOUT THE AUTHOR

1

How the Army Changed My Life

"Good," Captain Sargent said reviewing the row of young recruits. He stopped before me, "Not good."

"Sir?" I said raising a glass.

"I don't see legs, grunt."

"Yes, sir."

"Make legs."

"Yes, sir!"

"Show me your LEGS!"

To say I was intimidated by Captain Clarence Sargent was an understatement. The man stood six feet tall, had a fighting physique and his name contained two military ranks. "Sargent" was his family name—like the romantic painter, John Singer Sargent (no relation)—and the "Captain" referred to the highest position he'd held in the U.S. Army before he'd retired. Since he had been promoted to that rank, it meant there was a time in his life when he was called "Sergeant Sargent", which would have been hilarious if the 65 year-old Vietnam veteran had anything resembling a sense of humor.

Throughout college I had worked hard to "be all I could be" while not missing out on all the parties, so in the last semester of my final year I decided to take a less demanding academic course, what my university called "an elective" and I called a "blow-off". My academic advisor said this class should be on a subject that I was passionate about. I looked for classes on fashion, boys and keg beer parties but struck out.

"Here's something," she said pointing to the catalog on her desk. "A wine tasting class."

"I can study... drinking wine?" She nodded. I grinned.

Of course she neglected to say the instructor was Captain Sargent. If I had known that nugget of information I would have reconsidered. The first night of class the other students and I convened in a lounge-like room with sofas and armchairs. It was the most comfortable classroom I'd ever been in— until Captain Sargent arrived.

"This class is about wine tasting," he said, the overhead light giving his bald head a shiny glow. "So if you're here to suck down alcohol, cop a buzz, get loaded, tanked, wasted or otherwise inebriated, then hit the road Jack." He stopped before me, "And Jill." I gulped. "Wine is not a conduit to getting drunk. It's a manner of enjoying the finer things in life because it's one of the finest things in life."

On that first night we learned how to hold a glass. White wines are held by the stem with the fingers; red wines are held in the hand, which palms the ball of the glass, Sir! Because white wines should stay cool while drinking them and the mere heat from sweaty palms holding the beverage will raise the wine's temperature, Sir!

In the second class we learned to tell the age of red wine by looking at it. Hold the glass over a white tablecloth, white napkin or white marching orders, if the wine is a deep purple color it is young, Sir! If it's a lighter, brick red color it's older, Sir!

In the third class we got to swirl the wine in our glasses. Watching a man who ate Army recruits for breakfast swirl wine was one of the funniest things I'd seen, but then I have a sense of humor.

"You got a problem?" he said peering at me over his black-framed reading glasses.

"Swirling," I said. "It looks so snobby. Can't we just drink the wine?" His eyes met mine and in that instant I knew how the Viet Cong felt facing him on the battlefield—scared out of their skulls.

"Kid, you're revealing your immaturity and perpetuating tired old tropes while I'm talking science." He proceeded to explain how swirling the

3

wine in the glass is not snobby but necessary because it forces the liquid to bounce against the glass surfaces, which introduces air into the wine and helps increase its nose, flavor and all around pleasure. He warned us to be sure to swirl it enough to have the wine stream down the insides of the glass in long streaks or legs. "However," he said addressing me directly, "If you want to skip the 'snobby' swirl and guzzle it straight from the bottle, that's your business. But we'll see you're a fool." He then returned to his swirling.

To say he put me in my place was an understatement. That night something profound happened to me and my liver. We realized Captain Sargent was right. Wine didn't have to be snobby or stuck up. Instead it was something anyone with taste—which is not related to wealth or blue-blood status—could enjoy. And enjoying it meant I needed to spend more time with wine than I had with the beers I'd chugged to catch a buzz on Saturdays, Sundays and weekdays.

The following classes dealt with the great wine growing regions of the world—France, Italy and California—the history of their wines and what types of wines they made well today. I took notes during class, I reread my notes at home, I checked out library books on oenology, I swirled, sniffed, made legs and sampled. I studied harder for this course than any of my academic subjects, combined. Over his black-framed reading glasses, Captain Sargent noticed my resolve and classroom efforts but said nothing.

Our final exam and only grade was a pass-or-fail test administered individually. Each student was to be given a different wine and had to describe its essence and identify the grape varietal. Waiting in the hallway I paced, mentally running through my list of facts, figures and flavors. When my turn came I entered the lounge room where Captain Sargent sat at a table with an empty glass and several bottles concealed in brown paper bags. On his lap rested a small notebook. I sat facing him.

"Don't embarrass yourself, kid," he said grabbing a bagged bottle and pouring me a glass of white wine. I swirled the wine for aeration, I created legs a top model would envy, I inserted my nose in the glass and inhaled deeply.

"I smell apples — green ones," I said.

"Hmmm —"

"And melon... and maybe peaches?"

"No maybes. Be definitive." I sipped, sucked the wine through my teeth like he'd taught us and welcomed the fruits in my nose and mouth.

"Yes, peaches, definitely peaches," I said risking a smile. But the man who cut off his own finger to escape wartime imprisonment wasn't about to let me off the hook.

"Varietal?"

"Pinot... Grigio," I said gaining confidence with each word. "Which is the Italian version of what the French call Pinot Gris." I set the glass down. Was I correct? I didn't know. He made a mark in his notebook then waved me away.

5

I exited the lounge and wandered the campus aimlessly. Now was not the time to let a bad grade on a blow-off class affect my GPA. I needed to pass this class. But more importantly I wanted to pass it because I had developed a passion for it. Now I cared about wine, my liver and the finer things in life.

That Friday our grades were posted on the door to the lounge classroom. I located my student number and followed my finger across the page to the grade column. I passed!

To say that I was thrilled was an understatement.

I had grown to respect Captain Sargent and his oenological knowledge and although I realized we'd never be friends, he'd done something remarkable for me—he'd provided an introduction to wine and its pleasures, turning this college beer chugger into a passionate wine drinker.

All of which proves the old guy had a much better sense of humor than I thought. It also explains why I will forever be grateful to the Army.

2

Drinking Alone

"Look at those people sitting at outdoor cafés," I said walking down the cobblestone street.

"Talking, reading, drinking wine, it looks like they're having fun," I said back to myself in a very one-sided conversation.

One. It was a solitary number. The past few weeks I had been experiencing "one" *ad nauseam* that it had become the theme of my year: I had received *one* Fulbright scholarship to study in Belgium for *one* year to improve *one*self. Granted these were all positive things but there were negatives, too, since now I lived in *one* itty-bitty studio, a-*lone*, with money for *one*-half a person to survive on. My mother had discouraged me from taking this overseas gig. Her exact words were: "Are you crazy?"

To prove her wrong, I signed the contract and was now living in a busy foreign city, passing by outdoor cafés filled with people talking, laughing and drinking. It made me thirsty.

Perhaps I could meet up with a friend and we could quench our thirst together? That is if I had a friend in this town, country or anywhere east of Long Island. Half a world away I could hear my mother's voice: "I told you not to go live with all those foreigners."

Strolling through Brussels's sunny, 16th century Baroque square, I spied one man seated at a table with two chairs. Perhaps I could join him and we could consume a beverage together? But drink with a stranger? I could hear my mother's voice: "Over my dead body!"

My eye fell on an empty table with one chair. Perhaps I could sit and have a glass of wine by myself? But drink alone? In public? I could hear my mother's voice: "What are you, an alcoholic? What will people think?!" To my tea-totaling mother drinking was reserved for special occasions, like Thanksgiving, the Fourth of July and Christmas morning when we toasted to baby Jesus. All of this meant that to her, drinking alone was worse than gossiping, cursing or getting in a car accident wearing dirty underwear. A practical Midwesterner, she had strong opinions that even I, her wild and rebellious child, couldn't shake.

Weighted with my mother's words I by-passed the fun cafés, the delightful laughter and the delicious wine. Back at the university in my shoebox-sized studio, I pulled an unopened bottle of white wine from the refrigerator. I cradled it in my arms and looked at it longingly, then heard my mother's voice: "Anathema! Where's your self-respect? Only drunks drink alon—". Her words kept coming but I already knew where they went. Returning the bottle to the fridge, I ate a cold cheese sandwich and crawled into bed.

One was a very solitary number.

Throughout the following week I remained lonely and wineless. But on my walks through the city I noticed countless people—businessmen, young mothers, old men and ancient women—sitting alone in cafés, in bars or on sunny café terraces, and all of them were drinking alone. And most of them looked happy. All this solo imbibing meant that: 1) These people enjoyed wine; 2) They didn't mind being alone; and 3) None of them had a Midwestern American mother.

I noticed the profound cultural differences that denizens of my host country practiced, namely: Belgians had a royal family, spoke several languages and ate their French fries with mayonnaise not ketchup, now *that* was anathema. If I continued living with my American rules in Europe I wouldn't understand Belgian culture nor would I drink a drop of wine all year. In the spirit of cross-cultural Belgo-American understanding and major wine envy, I made a decision: I shed my

9

mother's warnings like a winter coat on the first day of spring. With purpose I marched to the café on Brussels's Baroque main square.

"Combien?" the waiter said grabbing four leather menus.

"Un," I said raising one finger indicating I would be alone, by myself, single, unaccompanied, flying solo and ready to face the shame of being called an "alcoholic". He returned three menus to his podium, then with a light step led me to the front of the outdoor terrace where he sat me at a pretty little table for one.

I lounged in the sun, I watched tourists pass by snapping their cameras—were they pitying me? Judging me? Who knew? I didn't care. I sipped my *vin blanc*. I gained confidence sitting alone and tasting the wine's floral finish on my tongue. Ahhh. So this is why Europeans don't mind drinking alone.

Sitting there I discovered tenets that even my mother could agree with: 1) Drinking wine alone was a great pleasure no matter which country you come from; and 2) If the wine is good, one is an outstanding number.

3

Beautiful Boxed Wine

"You made it!" my sister said greeting me at the airport terminal.

"That was the bumpiest, most-delayed cross-country flight ever," I said collapsing into her bear hug embrace.

"As soon as we get to the house I'll pour you a big glass of wine!"

Family: they're the only people in the world who really know what you need. Kay's comment made me forget the angst about the flight and look forward to the weekend's family reunion festivities and more importantly: that promised big glass of wine.

While her husband rolled my luggage into their home's spare bedroom, Kay and I retreated to the kitchen. With anticipation I watched as she seized two large goblets, opened the refrigerator and filled each one to the brim with... boxed wine.

Family: they're the only ones who never stop embarrassing you. Boxed wine? Had Kay lost her marbles? For the record, I adore my older sister for a lifetime of gifts and shared experiences. Growing up she showed me how to fold a fitted sheet, taught me how to shave my legs and explained what it meant when boys promised to call but never did. (Nutshell: They're jerks.)

However the days of her teaching me were long over and now it was up to me to return the favor. (Nutshell: Don't drink boxed wine.) Admittedly my experience with boxed wine was limited to a couple parties after college when the good times were rolling but the money was tight. My friends and I learned that we got more bang for our buck buying a 5-liter cardboard box of wine, plus—once it was empty—the box could double as a bedside table. (Nutshell: Money was really tight). Never mind the huge hangovers, that summer I drank so much sweet boxed wine that it rotted four of my teeth. After visiting the dentist I swore off the boxed brew preferring my wine bottled, sophisticated and with fluoride.

I confronted Kay about her boxed wine problem.

"Sis, I can't drink this."

"But it's good," she said smiling.

"*You* can't drink this," I said seizing her glass.

"But I like it. Don't you?" she said squinting her eyes. Now I'd hurt her feelings and there's nothing worse than hurting the hospitality feelings of your dear sister. Something had to be done. Someone had to be humored. I sniffed her wine. I swirled the honey colored fluid in her glass. I quaffed and I... enjoyed.

This white wine was good! Perhaps it was because the boxed wine industry had changed since my post-university days. Or perhaps wine makers had made a better recyclable box. Or perhaps it was because this box only held three liters, not five. Whatever the reason or combination thereof, I drank Kay's glass and my own and all weekend the entire family drank her boxed wine. It turns out that even as adults, we're still teaching and learning. (Nutshell: Don't judge a wine by its packaging.)

Family: they're the only people who keep you on your toes throughout your life.

4

Cool Chicks and Bottles

"I got so lost—" I stammered clutching my bottle.

"Not to worry," Isabella said smiling in the open doorway. "We've only just started." Like a presenter at the Oscars, she graciously steered me into her living room full of overstuffed sofas, uncorked bottles and well-coiffed ladies ready to drink.

Ah, the usual suspects.

This month my all girl wine group was sampling French whites. Traditionally French wines define themselves by the place where they're grown; or what is called their *terroir*. The French believe the soil, sunshine, fog, rainfall, hill slope, cloud cover and a myriad of other geographical elements affects how grapes grow and that eventually traces of these elements will end up in the bottle. The importance of *terroir* is why French labels don't list the grape varietal but the name of the region, sub-region, vineyard or *Chateau* What-Cha-Ma-Call-It where they're grown.

Despite having gotten lost in my own city and spending the past 30 minutes crisscrossing San Vicente Boulevard searching for Isabella's house with increasing panic, I was excited for the French geography tasting challenge. Bring it!

With French "location, location, location" the theme of the evening, the bottles in play included a Chardonnay from Burgundy, a Viognier from the Rhone River region, a bottle of Champagne from Champagne, and two bottles from the Loire Valley—a Sauvignon Blanc and a Chenin Blanc. My bottle of Riesling from Alsace was added to the mix.

We started by sipping my bottle from Northeastern France. Kari sucked wine and air through her teeth, sounding like a geriatric patient on life support.

"I taste the soil of Alsace," she announced.

"You do?" I said furrowing my brow.

"Oh, yeah," she continued. "I taste its cool, clay fields."

"Yes, darling!" Meredith bellowed in her Australian accent. "I taste the clay!" Shouts of "Me, too!" echoed from every drinker in the room except me. I didn't taste clay. I tasted… wine.

Before this night I'd already learned two wine facts: 1) Wine tasting was personal; and 2) Only I could say what my palate tasted. However, the purpose of joining a wine group was to train my palate to discern the different flavors in wines while sharing the findings with these amiable ladies. So it disturbed me that I couldn't pick out any of the Riesling flavors they claimed to have tasted.

The next bottle sampled was the Chardonnay from Burgundy. How intriguing to have a white wine grown in a region famous for reds. Eagerly I poured a glass.

"Darlings, I taste the fruit!" Meredith said smacking her lips. "The baked apple!"

"Don't forget the pear!" Kari said snapping her fingers.

"Yes! Baked apple and pear!" A chorus of "I taste it!" and "Me, toos!" sounded from every corner in the room. Every corner but mine. What was wrong? Why couldn't I taste the flavors? Was my tongue lazy? On vacation? Had the Indian curry I'd eaten for lunch zapped my taste buds? I seized a saltwater cracker from the cheese plate to cleanse my palate. Again I sipped the Chardonnay and this time I tasted… saltwater cracker.

The group sampled the next bottle. And the next.

"Delicious. I'm getting hints of soil," Kari said swirling the glass in the air. "And loam!"

"Yes, darlings, yes!" Meredith pounded the coffee table with her palm.

"Me, toos!" erupted from everyone in the room—every single woman—but me.

Among the ladies' chatter, I swirled the glass and sipped. I tried to taste its elements, the soil and the loam. Isabella leaned toward me.

"What do you think?"

"I'm completely lost," I said with a note of panic. Then lowering my voice to a whisper I said, "Do you know what 'loam' is?" Her eyes grew big. She looked me straight in the eye then burst out laughing.

"I haven't a clue!" She slapped her knee then we both got a fit of the giggles.

Since the night's wine tasting was lost to me anyway, I set my glass down and scooted next to Isabella on the sofa. One of the newer members of the group, all I knew about her was how devilishly hard her house was to find. Tuning out the other ladies, I listened and learned she was from Colorado, she worked as an ER nurse (her nursing certificate hung on the living room wall), and the African mask over the mantle was a souvenir she'd picked up in Zimbabwe while working there, on her vacation, as an ER nurse. The more I focused on her, the more I heard, saw and understood her.

"Oh, ladies! We can't forget the finale," Isabella announced pulling a bottle of Moet & Chandon Champagne from a bucket of ice. Kari handed out the flutes and Meredith popped the cork, which shot across the room like a cannonball.

"Finally, Darlings," she croaked, "The party's started!"

Toasting to Isabella, I heard our full glasses chiming like a church bell in a French country village. I watched the Champagne's air bubbles rise to the surface as if on a high-speed elevator only to disappear upon reaching it. I swallowed a mouthful. And another. Then incredibly—wonderfully—something happened.

"I taste…" I hesitated running my tongue over my lips. "I taste… lime."

"Yes!" Kari shouted.

"Bloody hell, that's good!"

"I love it!" Isabella said grinning at me.

"Me, too!" I said for the first time all night. "Me, too."

Then Isabella leaned in and whispered, "Do you know what '*lime*' is?" And we burst out laughing. We clinked our glasses and happily joined the other ladies in conversation.

Just when I thought I was a complete failure, I found the flavor and my self-confidence. In wine tasting it's not hard to feel lost or worse—ignorant—when you can't taste what others do. But that night I learned some new things: 1) Don't panic; 2) Focus on the wine; 3) Enjoy it with people you like.

5

Decanting Magic

"I brought the wine you asked for," my husband said setting the bottle on the kitchen counter.

"Excellent," I said rubbing my hands together with anticipation.

"It's young."

"Excellent."

"So young that when I bought it they were still stomping the grapes."

"Excellent!"

My husband looked at me as if I'd turned into Dr. Jekyll, Mr. Hyde and Frankenstein, simultaneously. My spouse deserved an explanation as to why I wanted one young bottle of wine, an eye of newt and toe of frog. But there wasn't time to explain, I had to begin my experiment.

Back in the Middle Ages people believed in vampires, dragons and alchemy. Alchemy, in case your pre-Renaissance history is a little rusty, is the proto-science of transforming everyday objects into super fabulous things. Alchemist experiments included turning nickel into gold, turning liquid gold into the fountain of youth and turning $5 on Kickstarter into a million bucks. While our Middle Ages' brethren were unsuccessful with their gold and fountain of youth projects, their descendants are making a mint on Kickstarter.

All this to say that I, too, was taking a page from our culture's collective alchemist past to turn something ho-hum into something howdy doody dandy! My experiment specifically entailed turning a young bottle of Cab into an older, refined *bouteille* of Cabernet Sauvignon, *s'il vous plait.*

I opened the recently purchased bottle of Cab and grabbed my empty decanter. Decanting a young wine is a one-step process of slowly pouring the bottled wine into a glass receptacle, or "decanter". This one move does several things: 1) It aerates the wine thereby bringing it in contact with oxygen; 2) This contact with oxygen improves the complexity of the wine; and 3) Decanting looks cool, making me feel like a witch with magical powers.

Then I conducted the hardest part of the experiment: waiting 20 minutes. I used the time to stir my cauldron, fly around on my broom and run a lint brush over my pointy black hat. (My black cat sheds everywhere.) Finally I shuffled into the living room with the decanter of wine and two glasses. I poured each of us a glass. My husband sniffed his, drank, then fell silent.

"Well?" I asked on pins and needles.

"For a young wine it's surprisingly... complex and delicious," he said.

"Ha, ha, ha!" I cackled.

Yes! My alchemy experiment worked! Actually the result of the aeration is not proto-science but real science for oxygen ages things—like people, food and cut flowers—and can turn a young wine into one that tastes several years older by giving it the attributes of increased subtlety, complexity and drinkability. This positive result proved to me that I could purchase young wines and make them older and better. My husband was totally on board with this.

Now I just had to tell him about my plans for that eye of newt and toe of frog...

6

Eiswein (aka Ice Wine)

"Merry Christmas!" my boss's wife said setting a festive wine bag on my desk.

"You shouldn't have," I said with a smile, then extracted a small, thin bottle. She saw the puzzlement on my face.

"It's a bottle of ice wine," she said.

"Uh-huh."

"It's made with frozen grapes."

"Uh-huh."

"It's one of the best things about Canada."

"…Uh…-huh."

Presents were the best—and worst—things about the holidays. The present pleasure—and the horrible crash and burn pain—were tripled when they related to your employer because the gift affected you, your employer and the employer's spouse, who was usually tasked with picking it out. This particular December I was working in Hollywood on an American TV show for a Canadian producer who, with his Canuck wife, saw it as their personal Maple Leaf loving mission to introduce me and every other sunny Californian on the show to the joys of "O Canada"! Most notably: ice hockey, ice fishing and now, ice wine.

Oh, you shouldn't have.

Don't get me wrong, the fact that my boss even thought about me during this festive season was a blessing. We'd all heard the horror stories about the nightmare boss who demanded that his assistant make his coffee, get his dry cleaning and sacrifice her weekends, her social life and both her blackberry pressing thumbs for the pleasure of working for said nightmare boss. Nope, the guy I worked for was nice, his wife was sweet and their high school-aged son was the kid brother I wished I'd had. They were the picture of the All-North-American family.

But clutching that small, slim bottle of alcohol, all I could say was "You shouldn't have", because I knew a thing or two about ice wine. 1) The Germans discovered *Eiswein* in the 19th century when a freeze struck their vineyards with the grapes still on the vines. 2) Frozen ice concentrated the grapes' sugars to make a sweet dessert wine. 3) Eiswein and ice wine sounded equally cold, forbidding and like something your mother used to make you drink for punishment.

"Young lady, you are not leaving the table until that glass of ice wine is empty!"

Although I knew something about ice wine, I had never drunk it because a bottle of the stuff would have cost me my monthly salary and the choice of paying rent won out over purchasing one bottle of ice wine. Nevertheless, it was hard to imagine that a freezing accident that had happened to some German vineyards in the 1830s could make its bottles twice the price of traditional table wines.

However thanks to the concept of supply and demand, I discovered there was some method to the pricing madness. The ice wine grapes hang on the vines for weeks or months after the usual harvest time for table wines just waiting for a nice freeze to zap them. But this longer time on the vine also increases the risk of the grapes falling off the vine or being eaten by birds, squirrels or ice hockey players before the freezing ice affects them. So a limited quantity means an increased price. Ta-da!

All this re-contemplation about ice wine had made me curious about the Canadian bottle in my gift bag. Over the Christmas holiday I made dinner for a friend and for dessert I unscrewed the half-bottle of ice wine.

"Fancy," my friend said rolling his eyes. "This little bottle is what you got? Are you sure your boss likes you?"

I raised the glass to my nose to inhale its aroma. Then I sipped, tasting its pear, apple and Canadian oak flavors. It was sweet, fruity and delicious. I was a convert. I raised my glass for a toast.

"To my boss and his wife: I said 'they shouldn't have' but I'm very glad they did."

That Christmas was sweet because I learned my boss liked me and that I liked ice wine. The only problem was the bottle was emptied too fast. So if you ever decide to buy ice wine for someone, splurge! And buy them a *whole* bottle because they'll want another glass!

7

Films about Wine, Fuggedaboutit!

I can't chase bad guy spies like James Bond. I can't scale Dubai skyscrapers on a "Mission Impossible" like Ethan Hunt. I can't fight evil in an "Ironman" suit like Tony Stark. But drinking wine with a couple of friends à la "Sideways", that—yes *that*—I can do.

When the movie "Sideways" (2004) came out it was a revelation. It showed that there were other wine regions in California besides Napa and Sonoma, it introduced the masses to Pinot Noir, and when "Miles" drank from the spittoon, it grossed out every person on the planet. Gross-out movie scenes are so memorable. Remember the one in "Trainspotting" when drug-addicted "Renton" sticks his hand into the dirty toilet then dives in?

I knew you would.

I think "Sideways" was such a hit because it was about regular people who liked wine and were trying to figure out their lives. That previous sentence describes 99% of the people I know, which means that my friends and I: 1) Have excellent taste in alcohol; 2) Are looking for love; or 3) Are balding and middle aged. We have so much in common.

So when a friend proposed taking a weekend trip to California's Central Coast wine region, I agreed. I brought my husband, Emily brought her spouse and an itinerary.

From her open car window Emily hollered, "First stop, the Hitching Post in Buellton, after that Fess Parker, then the Days Inn with the windmill!" Then she and George drove off.

My husband turned to me, "Really?"

Unfortunately the film's relatable-ness had spawned a cottage industry with tours of the locations used in the film. Going in person to The Hitching Post restaurant and the Days Inn hotel with the kitschy windmill let wine movie fans pretend— for a few moments at least—that they were in the movie. Apparently Emily was so gung-ho on experiencing every moment of the film during our couple's wine weekend, she had forgotten to inform us about this before we left.

"Well, here goes nothing," my husband said putting the car in drive. Once there but without reservations, Emily and George stood in line to get into The Hitching Post. Meanwhile my spouse and I went down the street and had a great meal at Pea Soup Andersen's. Despite Andersen's kooky billboards of two men splitting peas—or maybe because of them—their pea soup was delicious. While Emily and George grabbed a late lunch, we went to a local winery not on the itinerary and sampled some tasty Cabs and Pinots. While Emily and George waded through the swamp of tourists at Fess Parker Winery—the site of "Miles's" spit bucket quaffing scene—we bought several bottles to go and with our car found a quiet, shady place between the vineyards to enjoy the scenery and drink one of those Fess Parker bottles.

Emily texted, "Where are you?" I gave her our coordinates and soon after she and George arrived looking frazzled and beaten down.

"It was hard to do any wine tasting today with all those tourists," she said plopping down on our picnic blanket.

"Damn, tourists," George said kneeling beside her. I gave them glasses, my husband poured them our wine. In the late afternoon light we toasted each other and drank. Nothing soothes frazzled nerves better than a good glass of wine with friends. Emily and George relaxed, slowing down to our pace. The sunlight was warm on our skin, the sliced apples crisp, the wine full and warming. I cracked a joke about us being lousy tourists. We all laughed. It was a perfect moment.

George caught his breath and waving his hand around said, "This reminds me of something…"

"I know," Emily said. "It's like that cool scene in "Sideways" when the four of them are just hanging out and drinking together."

"That's it," said George.

Most people in the world remember the gross-out scenes in movies, but a few remember the beautiful, real scenes. I'm lucky to call those people friends.

8

Good Gifts

"Happy Christmas!" I said kissing Kari on the cheek under the mistletoe.

"I'm Jewish."

"Merry… Hanukah?" I whimpered.

Ahhh, December, that Most Wonderfully (Hectic) Time of the Year when we attend an endless string of parties celebrating Christmas, Hanukah, Kwanzaa, and according to the Mayan calendar, the complete destruction of the world. My women's wine group never met during the final month of the year because: 1) It was too crazy busy; 2) It saved us from giving gifts to our fellow wine group members; 3) We were serious shoppers and none of us liked forfeiting a night of shopping. Even for wine.

But this December we'd made time to meet because we'd found a useful theme: shopping for wine presents. Whoever had this idea (Kari), it was a stroke of genius!

The parameters of the evening were simple: 1) Bring a bottle of wine; and 2) Think outside the usual bottle.

We began with Nina's bottle of Veuve Cliquot, immediately recognizable by its canary yellow label. Its bright packaging was as classy as Tiffany's blue boxes and twice as expensive. The ladies in the group loved this Champagne and looked for any opportunity to bring a bottle, pop it open and suck it down. I supported this initiative and we all toasted to Nina for bringing the "Bubbly Widow".

"Who doesn't love Champagne?" Kari said sipping from her flute.

"What a bloody great gift for us," Meredith said in her throaty Australian accent.

"It's the gift we love to get," Nina said.

But not everyone on my Christmas list appreciated bubbles like we did and therefore shouldn't receive the Veuve. So we moved on to Kari's bottle, a Sofia Rosé by Coppola's Monterey Vineyards. The wine was fruity, made from Syrah and Grenache grapes and the Rosé gave the clear glass bottle a happy pink hue. It was the perfect gift for a woman who lived in a hot climate or who liked pink. A lot.

"Sweet," said Kari.

"It's a bloody good gift for a girl," said Meredith.

"It's a gift I'd like to give," said Nina.

But not everyone on my Christmas list was young and female. What about the men in my life? My colleagues? My *vino* drinking gal pals? So we moved on to Meredith's bottles from Rob Mondavi, Jr. The offspring and heir to Napa's Robert Mondavi had created a line of wines called ONEHOPE that donated a portion of the proceeds to specific charities. The bottle of ONEHOPE Zinfandel gave money to support the Troops, a Cabernet Sauvignon gave monies to Children with Disabilities and the Chardonnay donated money to Breast Cancer Research because women love their Chardonnay. What a fabulous idea! We could help charities by drinking wine. Those Mondavis were always thinking.

"Delicious and who doesn't love helping charities?" Kari said.

"What a bloody good gift for the needy," Meredith croaked.

"It's a gift I'd like to get," Nina smiled.

Seeming like we'd covered all the people on our lists I suddenly felt embarrassed about the present I'd brought. It was an Italian blend of Chardonnay and Pinot Grigio by Gaetano D'Aquino, which came in an oversized, colored bottle. The bottle was massive holding 1.5 liters of wine as opposed to the usual *petit* 750 milliliter size and the bottle's color was a unique blue. Brilliant blue. Lapis lazuli blue. Look at Me Blue!

"We shouldn't drink mine," I said self-consciously.

"Nonsense," Kari said opening the long-necked blue bottle and filling our glasses. In unison we sniffed and drank. Silence fell over our gifting group. Time stood still. After a full evening of imbibing delicious wines, mine tasted... flat. It was as if after the Three Magi gave baby Jesus gifts of gold, frankincense and myrrh, I schlepped into the stable and gave him my canteen of lukewarm well water.

"The wine is underwhelming," I said hurriedly.

More silence.

"But... the bottle is gorgeous!" Kari said admiring it on the table.

"The bottle! What a bloody great gift for a candle!" Meredith crooned.

"It's the gift my mother would love to get!" Nina said lifting the blue bottle to the light for closer inspection.

In unison we decided maybe it wasn't the best of the evening but everything has a redeeming factor. Once empty, the bottle could become a vase, a candleholder or a stunning conversation piece catching the light in a sunny window.

"For some folks," Meredith said, "Wine drinking is about more than what's in the bottle. And for some it's just the bottle."

How we laughed! Despite the hour we continued telling stories and chortling with each other.

Of all the holiday parties in the busy month of December, that was the best one because no one gave or received a tangible gift. Who among us needed *another* trinket? What made it so special was we were present, spending time together and drinking wine. On that December night I realized, that like the rest of the year, the greatest gift you can give your loved ones is your time.

9

Hybrid Wines
(aka Two are Better than One)

Have you ever visited New York City, London or Tokyo and said, "What a great city, I bet I could make it here!" Then you move there by yourself and suddenly you're overwhelmed by subway maps, "agonising" over funny British spellings and inundated with big-eyed anime characters. You realize you're not thriving in this new environment. In fact, you're barely hanging on, so before you wither and die there, you pack your bags and move back to where you came from.

That's how it was for wines.

Chardonnay, Syrah, Pinot Noir and many of the grape wine varietals that we know and love to drink are descended from one grand old grape plant called *Vitis vinifera*. *V. vinifera* can be found across Europe, North Africa and the Middle East but not in the Americas, which had their own indigenous *Vitis* varieties. North American grapes included among others: *V. labrusca, V. riparia* and *V. aestivalis rupestris*. Not exactly names that roll off the tongue, which is fitting since the wines made from them aren't as pleasing on the tongue either.

Eventually the European *V. vinifera* was brought to California where it thrived in the golden state's sunny Mediterranean climate, which led to Californians making American wines that could rival European ones. Winemaking remained concentrated on the Pacific Coast because other areas of North America—New York, Pennsylvania and Canada—were unable to grow Europe's heat-loving *vinifera* in their cooler climates.

Then disaster struck. In the mid-19th century a pest from North America—the phylloxera louse—was accidentally introduced to Europe where it destroyed that continent's *V. vinifera* vines. Then in the 1980s the louse was reintroduced to North America where it decimated *V. vinifera* on this continent while not harming the native North American varieties of *V. labrusca, V. riparia* and *V. aestivalis rupestris*. Researchers discovered if they grafted *vinifera* onto the roots of North American *Vitis* varieties, the plant would thrive and produce quality, *vinifera*-like fruit. *Voilà!* Two were better than one and problem solved!

Seeing the success of the grafting, East Coast researchers tried mixing strains of American and European grape varieties to create new vines that would thrive in the cooler, wetter climates of the Eastern seaboard and the Great Lakes Region. Known as "Hybrids" these varieties include the whites of Vignoles, Seyval Blanc and Vidal Blanc and the reds of Marechal Foch and Chambourcin. Without Hybrids we wouldn't have North American ice wines. In fact, Hybrids have helped spread winemaking to every American state and across Canada's provinces proving that two vines really are better than one.

Vitis vinifera needed American rootstock to survive in America and to make it on its own home turf of Europe, North Africa and the Middle East. Native North American vines needed the grapes of *V. vinifera* to make winemaking a trans-North American endeavor.

Have you ever visited New York City, London or Tokyo with a friend and said, "What a great city, I bet we could make it here together!" Then together you move there sharing a tiny apartment, splitting the rent and doubling your group of friends because you have your friends plus your roommate's friends. You work hard, make money and connections and suddenly you wake up one day and tell your roommate: "I made it because of you". And he says the same thing back.

That's how it is for wines today.

10

Italian Wines

"Teach me Italian," my friend Gloria said seated next to me on the train.

"But we'll be in Rome," I looked at my watch, "in ten minutes."

"Teach me something."

"Questa è deliziosa."

"...Delicious...-o."

Gloria was horrible at learning Italian and judging by the 136 pairs of shoes she'd toted along, she was even worse at packing. But on our maiden voyage to Italy she was excellent company because: 1) She's funny; 2) She likes wine as much as I do; 3) She is an Italian-American and even though she couldn't say, "Ragù pizza sauce", we got outstanding service because she looked more Italian than every other Italian we saw in Italy.

"Buon giorno, signorina!" The waiter sang brushing off a chair and holding it out for Gloria.

"What did he say?"

I sighed. "He said 'hello'."

"Oh!" she laughed. "Hello!" Her reply to the waiter only encouraged him, which meant throughout the meal I continued translating his endless compliments about her smile, her laugh, her beauty—*che bella!* The irony of the situation was that Gloria looked Italian—and hence was getting all the attention—but she couldn't speak a word of it. Meanwhile I, who did speak Fellini's language but looked to be any nationality except Italian, was ignored by every male within a 1,000 kilometer radius of Gloria.

Thankfully the wine was good.

For lunch on our first day we ordered pizzas and a couple glasses of Chianti, which is the standard Italian pizza lunch throughout the entire universe. But this Chianti was like no Chianti I'd ever had in the U.S. This Chianti had a full fruity flavor and hints of cinnamon and it came in a 750 milliliter bottle, not one of those fat, round bottles wrapped in a basket weave that hung from the ceilings of every pizza parlor west of the Atlantic Ocean. No, *signore*, this Chianti was delicious. I spoke to the waiter—interrupting him while he was singing Gloria's praises—to tell him how good the wine was.

"Naturalmente," he smiled and shrugged before returning his gaze to the deep brown orbs of Gloria's eyes.

The excellent Chianti-tasting campaign continued for dinner that night and the following day's lunch and dinner, and the day after that. At every restaurant I ordered Chianti wishing for the winning streak to carry on, but knowing human nature, realized one of these Chiantis had to fail soon. But they didn't. Each Chianti was as delicious as the next. It was an incredible winning streak—better than the Lakers under Phil Jackson, better than the Dodgers with Jackie Robinson, better than the Yankees in the World Series!

But how? In my uneducated U.S. experience, Chianti was a cheap table wine trying hard to be a cooking wine. Actually, Chianti refers to a type of wine grown in the Italian region of Florence. Traditionally it is a combination of three Italian grapes: Sangiovese, Canaiolo and Malvasia Bianca. But the quantities and qualities of these grapes could fluctuate because Chianti vintners are a diverse bunch. So how could I explain all the different, tasty Chiantis we'd drunk?

After two weeks in Rome and Florence I discovered the answer: Italians like Italian things, which they want to keep all to themselves. This explained why they were fawning all over Gloria. Each one of those mambo *italianos* was hoping to entice her to stay in Italy with him. It also explained why I'd never tasted a good Chianti outside of Italy.

I bet they export the so-so Chianti but keep the good stuff for themselves.

On our last night in Rome, Gloria and I ate outside at the Piazza Campo dei Fiori. The background music was cheesy romantic, the pasta was savory and the Chianti did not disappoint. Holding up her wineglass, Gloria pulled on my sleeve.

"How do you say 'This is delicious'?"

"Questa è deliziosa."

"… Questa—" she stammered.

"E deliziosa," the waiter said finishing her sentence.

"Naturalmente," I replied. And for the first time I received the waiter's look of approval.

11

Jesus, the Winemaker

Jesus and his disciples were invited to a wedding at Cana. The mother of Jesus was there, too. When they ran out of wine, the mother of Jesus said to Him, "They have no wine."

Jesus said to her, "What does your concern have to do with Me? My hour has not yet come."

His mother said to the servants, "Whatever He says to you, do it."

Now there were set there six waterpots of stone, according to the manner of purification of the Jews, containing twenty or thirty gallons apiece. Jesus said to servants, "Fill the waterpots with water." And they filled them up to the brim. And He said to them, "Draw some out now, and take it to the master of the feast." And they did. When the master of the feast had tasted the water that was made wine, and did not know where it came from (but the servants who had drawn the water knew), the master of the feast called the bridegroom. And he said to him, "Every man at the beginning sets out the good wine, and when the guests have well drunk, then the inferior. You have kept the good wine until now!"

This beginning of signs Jesus did in Cana of Galilee, and manifested His glory; and His disciples believed in Him. (John 2:1-11, New King James Bible.)

Jesus made winemaking look easy, but it's not.

Jesus made winemaking seem like a miracle, but it's science.

Jesus made wine without tasting it, which *is* a miracle!

Even before Jesus's wedding feat turning water into wine, winemakers strove to create drinkable wine. In the earliest days of winemaking (6,000 BCE) tree sap, or resin, was added to wine to prevent it from becoming vinegar. In ancient Greece, Pliny the Elder wrote about the numerous different tree saps that could be added to wine and which ones he preferred. In fact, in his writings, he detailed more about the saps than the grapes.

But the grapes are where the process starts. Grapes are harvested in the fall. Fruit that will make

48

white wine is de-stemmed and de-skinned and put into vats to ferment. Grapes that will make red wine are de-stemmed and put into vats with their skins still on. For both white and red wines, yeast is added to the vats and this yeast converts the grape juice sugars into alcohol. This process takes a couple weeks, which already is longer than the entire wedding *and* honeymoon at Cana.

Throughout these steps the winemakers are continuously sampling the white and red wines to make them tasty and distinctive. They can change or enhance the flavor of a wine while it's still in the vats by adding or blending the juice of other grapes to it. Unlike Jesus, they never mix water with the wine. No sane person mixes water and wine.

The red grape skins are separated from the red wine liquid, then the red grape juice is transferred to oak barrels for a second fermentation. While resting in these barrels, the red wine will pick up flavors from the oak barrels. White wine can be aged in oak barrels or stainless steel ones. Unlike the Cana wedding, no one these days stores wine in stone waterpots.

After weeks, months or years of this fermentation step—and lots of agonizing by the winemakers, "Is it good enough? Will it get better? Will it get worse?"—the wine is transferred to bottles, labeled and shipped to a store near you. Unlike in Cana, a servant won't make a personal delivery.

After purchase, you'll open the bottle, pour a glass and hopefully—if the winemakers have done their jobs right—you'll say "I've kept the good wine until now!" Which is *exactly* like they did at the wedding in Cana.

For wine lovers it's heartening that Jesus's first miracle was making wine, but wow, he sure made the process look easy for every other winemaker who's followed him; when it's not.

12

Kosher Wine

A minister, a priest and a rabbi walk into a winery and the minister goes up to the winemaker and says, "I've come to taste your dry white wine." The winemaker pours her a glass and the minister days, "Delicious."

The priest goes up to the winemaker and says, "I've come to taste your dry red wine." The winemaker pours him a glass and the priest says, "Delicious."

The rabbi goes up to the winemaker and says, "Where's the closest juice bar?"

During certain times of the year, including Passover and the Sabbath, observant Jews are required by their religion to drink kosher wines. Since the 19th century the kosher wines favored by American Jews have been stigmatized for being overly sweet and having a low alcohol content. "Kosher wine" refers to the manner in which the wine is made, specifically religiously observant Jewish men are involved in every step of the winemaking process including: harvesting the grapes, fermenting the grapes and bottling the wines.

With the American Jewish populations traditionally concentrated in the New York metropolitan area and the Midwest, these groups made kosher wines with grapes grown in those areas, most commonly the dark blue Concord grape. A *Vitis labrusca*, the Concord is indigenous to North America and known for its bold, sweet juice; not its aroma, subtlety or acid (read: alcohol content). Since 1927 the sweet Concord/*labrusca* grape has been used to make Manischewitz's kosher wine, which contains additives—corn syrup or agave syrup—to further sweeten the brew. In addition, the brand's alcohol content was one of the lowest at just 11%. It's Manischewitz that gave kosher wines the moniker "too sweet", "grape juice" and "bug juice for grownups".

In recent years the kosher wine market has expanded beyond Manischewitz and now includes vineyards that have sprung up in Israel, France and California. Vintners at these establishments are using *Vitis vinifera* grapes, which includes varieties such as Cabernet Sauvignon, Syrah and Grenache, to make quality kosher wines that are dry with hints of oak, tannins and subtle fruit flavors with an alcohol content ranging from 13%-15%. In other words, they're making anything but bold, sweet wines. And the liquid merchandise is flying off the shelves. American Jews are voting with their wallets: they want more than sweet grape juice; they want good wine.

These new wineries and winemakers may make the rabbi reconsider his request.

The rabbi goes into a winery and says to the winemaker, "Give me some of your kosher Cabernet." The winemaker pours him a glass and the rabbi says, "Ahhh. So *this* is wine!"

13

Languedoc-Rousillon, Spain

"Want to spend our honeymoon in France's wine country?" my newlywed husband asked over breakfast.

"I do!"

The most unusual wedding gift we received was from my husband's work colleague, Philippe: a week's stay at Philippe's family's second home in the Languedoc-Rousillon region of southern France. The information was handwritten on a pretty, paper wedding card with straightforward instructions: when we'd decided on a week, Philippe would give us the house key. When we returned, we'd give the key back to him. It was so simple. This was going to be the best honeymoon ever!

At the time we were living in Belgium, we'd had a winter wedding and I'd just changed jobs to avoid a jerky employer. You know the type: jerky with a capital "J". So we pushed our honeymoon to the summer when we would both be in the mood for celebrating our marriage and the weather would be in the mood to regale us with sunshiny days and romantic nights.

We notified Philippe of our dates, he gave us the house key, the directions and wished us well. My husband and I looked at the metal latchkey and giggled like school kids who'd cut class without the teacher finding out. What a great wedding gift!

With our bags stowed in our *petite* Peugeot, we drove south to the French border, around Paris, south on the E15 and the *autoroute du soleil,* which took us to Provence but we kept driving south. Once we hit the Mediterranean we turned right, passed through the city of Perpignan and entered a hilly region marked by medieval-era stone villages and row after row of vineyards. This was Languedoc-Rousillon.

Languedoc-Rousillon is the largest wine-producing region in France. Throughout the twentieth century it was the largest wine-producing region in the world. Whenever you are in Paris, Marseilles or Brussels and you see a *vin de Pays d'Oc* on the menu, those wines come from this region. The soil of the Languedoc-Rousillon is limestone, which makes the grapes work for their moisture to produce a quality fruit. Although this region built its reputation on table wine and *vin de pays*, the last few years new Languedoc-Rousillon wineries have been producing higher quality vintages with higher prices. I was hoping to taste all these varieties during our week in the area.

After passing the correct number of stone villages, vineyards and cafés, we turned at the "big rock" and entered a dirt driveway, which was lined with lush grape vines. The drive veered right to reveal a small, charming stone house in the middle of a vineyard. Already this was the best honeymoon ever!

We unlocked the door and stepped inside. Even with the loft it wasn't a large space but for the two of us for one week, it was perfect. My husband turned on the generator for the electricity, I unloaded our bags, and up in the loft, I put our clean sheets from home on the bed. Then we locked up and drove to a nearby medieval village to buy a week's worth of food supplies and dinner.

That night we ate pasta and drank *vin de Pays d'Oc*. Maybe it was my imagination, or maybe it was my built-up anticipation finally becoming reality, or maybe it was my happiness over the best honeymoon ever that was enhancing the flavor but the wine that night was so flavorful: berry fruit forward with a dry, full finish. I can still taste it now.

Across the table I made googly eyes at my husband. He made googly eyes back. This was our honeymoon and we were both ready for some honey. In the dark night he drove our Peugeot like a Formula 1 racecar driver through that old village—squealing tires and all—back to our charming stone house in the vineyard.

As we turned the corner of the driveway and approached the house, we stopped in the darkness. In front of our honeymoon bungalow we saw... another car.

"Are you expecting someone?" I asked my husband.

"Not on my honeymoon."

"Maybe it's a neighbor?"

"It's 11 o'clock at night. Besides, the car has Belgian license plates."

"All our stuff's inside," I said with panic. "Go find out who it is!"

"Why me?!"

Marriages, no matter how new, are compromises. As he approached the house with the key, I found a stick of wood on the driveway and, hoisting it over my head, followed him to the front door. He unlocked the door only to find a blond man and woman sleeping in the loft, in our honeymoon bed, on our clean sheets.

Apparently Philippe had given us his key to the family's little house in the vineyard and unbeknownst to him, his parents had given their key to their friends' daughter for her school vacation, which was the exact same week.

Two couples, two vacations, one house in a vineyard. It was so complicated. Agreeing to sort things out in the morning, we slept on the lumpy, sofa bed downstairs all the while hearing the blond Belgians sawing wood in the loft over us.

In the morning I went running along the vineyards and through another medieval village with chickens crossing the road and geraniums bursting with crimson blooms. Languedoc-Rousillon was quiet, beautiful and the perfect place for a honeymoon. I hoped we could find a resolution with the other visitors.

At the local village my husband bought fresh pastries for breakfast. While munching on our croissants, the Belgians told us they didn't care that we'd arrived before them; they didn't care that we'd turned on all the utilities and made the bed with our sheets; they didn't care that we were wine lovers and they weren't; and they really didn't care that this was our honeymoon. They'd decided: they were staying.

It was now the worst honeymoon ever.

We could've booked a hotel in one of the neighboring villages but the thought of running into those rude blondes convinced us otherwise. Besides the world is a big place. So we packed our things—including the dirty bed sheets—and drove south over the Pyrenees Mountains into Spain, only stopping once we'd arrived in Barcelona. There we saw Gaudí architecture together, we walked Las Ramblas together, we drank Spanish *vino rioja* together. It was so simple and beautiful. For a honeymoon, that's all you need: wine and being alone together. It was the best honeymoon ever. Truly.

The wines of Languedoc-Rousillon are wines of flavor, wines of romance and wines that I will forever associate with... Spain.

14

Moscato Wine

"Enjoy your trip to wine country today," I said pouring coffee for our guests.

"Come with us," Stephen said in accented English.

"I have to work—"

"*'In no time it's the present'*, as you Americans say."

"That's not the expression—"

But he wasn't listening.

Stephen and his Dutch girlfriend, Mimi, were visiting us in our tiny one-bedroom apartment in Marin County, California. Marin is famous for redwood trees, George Lucas's Skywalker Ranch and for being "God's Country"—that fertile patch of land north of San Francisco and south of Sonoma County. Marin has sunny days, cool nights and a totally relaxed vibe that means all its residents wear flip-flops every day, everywhere. Since it's one of the wealthiest plots of earth on earth, all Marin flip-flops are made of solid gold. Of course.

Marin's location, sandwiched between one of the hippest cities on the planet and one of the finest wine regions of the world, means residents brag about its proximity to these locations nonstop yet rarely visit them. Our landlord moved to Marin during the Johnson Administration and hadn't left the county since the Summer of Love. It was like life-long New Yorkers who have never visited the Statue of Liberty because who would choose to go elsewhere when it was so good at home? No one. Of course.

Although we lived in the county's only affordable town—what I called "Workingman's Marin"—and our annual salaries were mere pocket change for 99.99999% of the county's residents, after a few months of living there, my newlywed husband and I had been infected with the "Marin is God's Country" ethos. We relished exploring the area as long as it meant we stayed within the confines of our county. As a Dutchman, Stephen wasn't having any of it. He'd traveled halfway across the globe to see us and wine country and he wanted to see us *and* wine country at the same time.

So on a July day when the temperature was a perfect 85 degrees Fahrenheit in Marin, Stephen,

Mimi, my husband and I left God's Country for Sonoma. Driving north we felt the heat outside our air-conditioned car increase until it hit triple digits. Arriving in Sonoma City we wanted to get out and explore the old central square, its charming shops and tony restaurants, but the heat was so intense that we skipped town altogether and high-tailed it to a winery.

If I said it was "hot" at Ravenswood Winery it would be an understatement. Leaving our air-conditioned car I stood on the driveway and felt my physical energy disappear faster than leather handbags at a half-off sale. Despite my wide brimmed hat and flip-flops, the oppressive oven-like air beat down on me like a relentless heavyweight champ. A thermometer read 106 degrees. We left God's Country for *this?!*

The tasting room was jam-packed with tourists happily clamoring to taste the red wines that Ravenswood is famous for. Despite the boiling temperatures, Stephen and Mimi joined the thirsty hordes in drinking full-flavored Zinfandels and robust Cabernet Sauvignons. But not me. That day was too hot for red wine: I couldn't drink it, discuss it or even think about it. Instead I needed something white and cool. Anything white and cool. I said I'd even take a bucket of dirty pool water. The tasting room pourer laughed and let us sample Ravenswood's Moscato Leggero.

Moscato is a class of grapes—purple, green or white—traditionally grown in Italy for sweet summer wines. If anyone knows what wine to drink in hot weather, it's the Italians. On my tongue the Moscato tasted sweet, crisp and fruity (hints of honeysuckle? Apricot?). Although it was sweet, it didn't get bogged down by the weight of its own fruit. Instead it was delicious and refreshing. Sipping it I felt energy returning to my body, my brain, my soul.

First my body cooled down. Then my brain bought a case of it. Then my soul exclaimed: This—*this!*—was why we left Marin: to discover Moscato so I could forever fall in love with it! Of course!

For me, wines are like shoes because the weather dictates your choice for both. Flip-flops are worn every day in Marin because it's always 85 degrees and sunny. But for the rest of the world, you wouldn't wear heavy boots in the middle of the summer nor would you wear flip-flops in the snow. Likewise I won't drink a big Zinfandel or Cabernet Sauvignon on a triple digit, hot day because on those days I'll be drinking Moscatos.

After lunch, our sweltering foursome returned to our Marin apartment and immediately cooled off by jumping into the complex's swimming pool. The rest of the afternoon we lounged beside our heavenly lagoon sipping ambrosial Moscatos because as we say in God's Country, "*In no time it's the present.*"

Of course.

15

The Nose

"Those jeans are amazing."

"Your hair cut is amazing."

"Your cuticles are freakin' a-ma-zing! OMG!"

Lately people I know—mostly myself—have been over-using the word "amazing", putting it in simple sentences about everyday life. Last week I was talking to my husband.

"The metro comes in two minutes? Amazing!"

According to the dictionary, "amazing" means "to cause surprise or great wonder" and the word's been around since 1593 when Shakespeare created it to "amaze" his early poem "Venus and Adonis". Since that literary work is about a god and a goddess having divine intercourse, I'm pretty sure "amazing" was never meant to be used in the context of mere mortals, our quotidian life or any of our personal grooming successes, no matter how great that manicure was.

Many Americans—maybe just me—use "amazing" in a manner similar to the way the British use "brilliant".

"Your posture is brilliant."

"Your scarf is brilliant!"

"That whisk is bloody brilliant! Blimey!"

The other day I was speaking to my British friend Evie trying to organize a movie night.

"I'll call you tomorrow," I said.

"Brilliant!" Evie bellowed.

A phone call is not "brilliant" unless you are referring to the whole process of how our phones now can be used to make calls—without wires—anywhere on earth or 30,000 feet above it, take pictures, send messages and complete an entire university degree faster than three finger snaps, after which we just slide the thing back into our pocket. Now *that,* I grant you, is truly brilliant and amazing.

But me calling you? That's just humdrum life. By overusing "amazing" and "brilliant" we're cheapening the really amazingly brilliant things in our world, like my friend's nose.

Everyone says—okay, just me—that Kari's nose is amazing. Luckily Kari and I are in the same wine group so I have seen her schnauz up close and personal for years. Watching her stick her facial protuberance into the glass and inhale half its liquid contents is one of the highlights of our get-togethers. She is not dainty about it. She just pokes it in there and sucks in air like a reverse jet-propulsion vacuum cleaner. You have to see it to believe it.

Since the 1990s wine tasting has increased in popularity, yet this "tasting" is a misnomer. The human tongue can only detect a limited number of tastes, which are: sweet, sour, salty, bitter, acid and savory. This is far from amazing.

With such a limited range for the tongue, wine "smelling" increases in importance. The human nose contains an olfactory bulb in the lower, front part of the brain that can detect numerous different scents, smells and odors, some of which include (drum roll): fruits (apple, blackberry, apricot, cassis, melon), flowers (rose, geranium, orange blossom), earth (mushroom, dust, mold, dampness), citrus (grapefruit, lemon, lime), vegetal (bell pepper, hay/straw, asparagus, freshly cut green grass), mineral (stone, gravel, rock) and many more amazing scents. With the nose's power and range of detectable smells, it only makes sense to smell the wine before drinking it so as to enhance the tongue's taste of it.

Beyond the comical spectacle that is Kari's nose smelling a wine's aroma, I have witnessed how her nose works discerning scents, smells and odors.

I smell eucalyptus," she said about a Shiraz. "I'm getting honeysuckle," she said about a Viognier. "I'm picking up cinnamon sticks," she said about a Grenache. Amazing. After she named each fragrance she detected, I smelled my wine and I got the same fragrances. Her nose is amazing! Could I detect any specific aromas before Kari does? I don't know, her nose is always stuck in the glass before mine.

Everyone tells Kari—actually, just me—that she and her honker should get a job as a sommelier, a perfume creator or as a mom because if anyone needs a good nose to determine if the milk is sour, the eggs are bad or the wine is good, it's a mom.

Kari just laughs and says she's happy with her life just as it is. She especially likes smelling and drinking wine with everyone in our group. With that, she raises her glass and toasts to us. That woman and her nose are brilliant and amazing! Which is what everyone says—them and me—about her together.

16

Oak Barrels,
Another Breed of Cat

When making wine, there's more than one way to skin a cat. These days winemakers can use various techniques to create a quality *vino* for the market. One of the most versatile elements in the winemaker's tool kit is oak.

Oak barrels have been used to store and ferment wine since at least the Roman times, thus becoming the cat's meow of storage vessels. The wine industry is slow-changing so it has continued to embrace this oak technology the way a young husband clings to his video games and concert t-shirts.

While serving as a storing/fermenting vessel, oak's inherent properties interact with the wine, imparting the wine with flavors of vanilla, butter, wood, toast, caramel, spice, smoke and/or fruit. It can also soften a wine's tannins. In case you're as curious as a cat, tannins are plant compounds found in the skins, stems and seeds of grapes, (that are used in making red wine), which when found in abundance can cause your mouth to become dry and pucker after drinking *vin rouge*. Having some tannins in red wine is vital for wine to be aged and for imparting body to the wine as it lays in the taster's mouth. Therefore oak is often used to age these tannins, which can smooth out a red wine's flavor, preventing it from being too astringent and mouth puckery. It also keeps the cat from getting your tongue.

The biggest suppliers of oak barrels are: 1) North America, which uses American White Oak wood; 2) France, which uses European White Oak or Common Oak; and 3) Hungary, which uses Common Oak, which is variously called Hungarian, Italian, Balkan or East European Oak. American oak has a looser wood grain, which allows it to have a quicker effect on the wine it holds. Vintners often use American oak barrels to create bold Cabernets or buttery Chardonnays or they can use the more finely grained French or Hungarian oak barrels for a longer period of time to nurture more subdued wines that sneak up on you like a cat.

Some French vineyards are so proud of fermenting their wines in oak barrels they mention it on the label: *Élevé en fût de chêne*, which means "aged in oak barrels", if you forgot your high school French back in high school.

Some French winemakers like American oak barrels. Some Americans like French oak ones and all Canadians like Canadian oak barrels. It's the only time Canadians prefer any tree over the Maple.

Oak barrels are expensive to purchase yet most only hold 59 gallons of wine—in other words, 295 bottles—and are only used for three to five years, at which time the benefits of the oak have been leeched out of the wood and the barrel is defunct for wine but suddenly perfect for planting pink petunias. Clearly oak barrels don't have a cat's nine lives.

Some winemakers age their wines in stainless steel tanks but can still add an oaky flavor with thin oak chips. The chips impart wood characteristics to the wine faster than barrels do, helping to shorten their fermentation times and get the wines to market faster, thereby making a vineyard owner grin like a Cheshire cat.

So the cat's out of the bag: in the wine world, oak is the coolest cat around.

17

Pregnant (and Not) Wine Tasting

"Taste this Châteauneuf-du-Pape," my husband said pushing his wine glass toward me.

"No, thanks."

"It's delicious."

"No, thanks."

"Just a sip?"

"No, thanks!"

I love wine. And unlike gin, vodka or shots of worm-infused tequila, wine loves me back. But when I got pregnant, I stopped drinking wine, sipping wine, tasting wine. My husband was devastated.

"How will I know what's good?" he said with alarm.

"You will learn."

Ever since we'd started dating, whenever my husband and I would go to a restaurant the waiter would seat us, give us menus then hand my husband the wine list, which he promptly slid across the table to me. In our two-some I was the gal who ordered the wines and he was the guy who paid for them. It was a good relationship.

Most doctors agree that if pregnant women drink a sip of wine on a special occasion it will not hurt the fetus. Meanwhile all doctors agree that going on an alcoholic binge-bender for 16 days, snorting cocaine and smoking meth will hurt the fetus. A lot.

For myself I decided not to drink during that time hoping to: 1) Have a healthy child; 2) Refresh my taste buds after the pregnancy; 3) Remind my husband how much he needs me. I was just thinking of my family.

But I had a Groupon to a wine bar near the beach that was about to expire. So after work one night we rendez-vous'ed at said wine bar with said Groupon. The Italian waiter greeted us with his charmingly crooked smile, handed us menus and gave *me* the wine list, which I promptly slid across the table to my husband. He freaked.

"They have so much! What do I order?" he said flipping through pages of *vinos*.

"Start with what you like."

He sampled a Sauvignon Blanc. It was crisp and refreshing but with the ocean breezes perhaps a little too cool for this late dinner. I encouraged him to switch to red.

He sampled a Pinot Noir. I showed him how to swirl the glass on the table, which: 1) Would aerate the wine thereby adding depth to its flavor; and 2) Would make him look like he knew what he was doing. He swirled like a pro. The people seated at the table next to us commented that my husband really looked like he knew what he was doing. They all started swirling like him. He looked at me with shock.

"I told you," I said eating my wine-less wild mushroom soup.

He grew confident. He sampled a Syrah from Santa Barbara County, a Pinot Noir from Oregon, and a Bordeaux from... well, Bordeaux, France. I asked him which flavors he tasted. His tongue rolled in his mouth and he said he could taste: "fruit, plums, light tannins, round, soft, full". Slightly slurring his words, he proclaimed that all the wines were good for consumption and since he didn't pour any of the samples out, I believed him.

He ended the night with a Châteauneuf-du-Pape. The aroma, the aeration, the swirl, he had it all down. Then he drank his glass.

"Delicious."

"You've learned so much you don't need me anymore," I said.

"Oh, I need you. I need to tell you exactly what you're missing out on," he said swirling his glass in my face. I laughed. If the shoe were on the other foot and he were pregnant, I'd do the same thing to him.

It was a very good relationship.

18

Quench Your Thirst in
Las Quintas

"I'm planning our vacation," I said pulling my husband toward my desk.

"Okay."

"We're going on a wine tour."

"Okay."

"To see Las Quintas!"

"… Huh?"

My husband was a smart fellow so I didn't blame him for not knowing about Las Quintas of Portugal. Most Americans were more familiar with

La Quinta Inns, the budget hotel chain located along a freeway near you, than with Portugal's exquisite wine country. But I was going to change his world.

Wines are grown on estates, which are called *chateaux* in France, *villas* in Italy and ranches in California. In Portugal they're called *quintas* and in one region of that country, *quintas* and grape vines predominate: the Douro River Valley.

The Douro River originates in north central Spain and runs west to Portugal where, at the city of Porto, it empties into the Atlantic Ocean. For millennia this river has carved its path through steep mountains of granite and limestone to reach its destination. For three centuries Portuguese farmers cut into the mountains to plant terraced rows of grape vines. For seven days my husband and I would experience it!

Douro River Valley grapes—Tinta Roriz (aka Tempranillo), Touriga Franca, Touriga Nacional, Tinto Cão, Tinta Baroca as well as Gewürztraminer, Sauvignon Blanc and Cabernet Sauvignon—"like" the rocky soil because it makes them struggle for water and nourishment. It's an ideal climate for grape growing, with half the region's fruit used to make table wines and the other half made into Port.

Port? That pretentious sounding Before or After Dinner drink favored by the Victorian era's upper class? Yep, *that* Port. Like Porto, the city where the Douro meets the ocean? Yep, *that* Porto. Coincidence? I think not!

Unlike table wine, Port is a "fortified wine", which means the grapes are planted, grown and harvested just like they are for table wines. However during the fermentation process *aguardente*—a type of sweet grape brandy—is added to the fruit juice to stop it from fermenting in order to create a sweeter beverage yet one with a higher alcoholic content. These days most table wines contain anywhere from 11%-15% alcohol content while Port can have a whopping 18%-22% alcohol content. Port is a sweet drink that gives a major buzz. Ah-hah, smart! That's why the Victorians drank it!

Most *quintas* grow and produce table wines and fortified wines. The last 20 years the Douro River Valley has seen a boom in table wine production and tourism so that it is now on the radar for alcohol lovers. Coincidence? I think not!

Although most *quintas* are owned by large corporations, a number of smaller *quintas* have retained grape production while being converted into hotels where wine tourists like my husband and I could eat, drink and be very merry.

Explaining all this to my husband I noticed his eyes had glazed over, so I cut to the facts.

"We'll fly to Portugal and after experiencing Porto, we'll start our wine tour at Quinta do Côtto, a working, licensed vineyard since 1757, which now has a restaurant on its grounds. Then we'll go to the modern Quinta do Portugal, which offers tours of the wine making production in its winery building designed by Pritzker Prize-winning architect, Siza

Vieira. Finally, we'll unwind at Quinta Nova Nossa Senhora do Carmo by hanging out at its swimming pool located amongst its rows and rows of terraced grape vines." I paused for breath. "What do you think?"

My husband hesitated. I panicked. Did I plan too much? Did I plan too little? Had he stopped liking wine? Then he spoke.

"Any of these places offer wine samples?"

"They all do."

"I'm in."

Like the Victorians, my husband was a smart fellow.

19

Retsina at the Parthenon

"Welcome to Greece!" my cousin, Mike, said embracing me.

"This calls for a celebration," my husband said hugging Mike.

"I know just the place to go," Mike said.

Nothing unites family like bone-crushing hugs and a celebratory drink. With the former accomplished, it was time to move on to the latter. My husband and I were on our first visit to Greece and at that exact same time my cousin, the Marine, was stationed in Athens. How unique to meet Mike halfway around the globe in one of the most beautiful, historically significant cities of the world. I got a chill just walking along the Parthenon down the same cobblestone streets as Plato, Socrates and Maria Callas—if that opera star ever walked.

That evening we met up with Mike and his Marine Unit's Commanding Officer (CO). Since Mike was going out with civilians for pleasure, military policy required his CO to accompany us as a sort of chaperone. It didn't matter to me—"the more the merrier" was my motto!—just as long as I could share a celebratory drink of Retsina with my family.

Retsina is Greece's traditional wine and it's hard to avoid when there. Retsina uses white Savatiano or Assyrtiko grapes to make a white wine or sometimes it uses the pink Rhoditis grapes to make a Rosé. No matter the color, what makes a Retsina a Retsina is that it is flavored with the sap (aka resin) of the Aleppo pine tree. Yes, pine tree sap is *purposefully* added to the wine must during fermentation, giving the wine a—how do I say this nicely?—a pungent, paint-thinner, turpentine-like nose. Upon reflection, this smell may explain why Retsina is not often found outside Greece.

Over 2,000 years ago Retsina was drunk by the ancient Greeks. That classical era was a time before glass bottles or corks, so wine was stored in thin-necked clay amphorae with each amphora sealed with pine resin to prevent the wine from spilling or souring. Needless to say some of the pine resin mixed with the wine and Greeks have been drinking tree sap with their wine ever since.

None of this mattered to me—"When in Athens do as the Athenians do" was my motto!

Besides I knew just the place to go. I wanted to drink Retsina with Mike and my husband while sitting at a café gazing up at the Parthenon.

Unfortunately Mike's CO had other plans.

"I know just the place to go." The CO announced that he was taking us to a "great bar that served the best Greek beer you've ever had." The three of us agreed because… he was the CO.

The CO marched us into the historical district and as soon as we caught sight of the elegant Parthenon perched on the hill, promptly turned us into a maze of Athenian streets zigging and zagging until we reached a small café. The Parthenon was blocked from our view, in fact everything was blocked from our view except a couple of flea-ridden cats sprawled on the cobblestones. But it didn't matter to me—"The celebratory drink with family show must go on" is my motto!

The CO ordered the "best" beer known to humankind for the three men and I ordered a glass of Retsina. Unfortunately this was the only café in Athens that didn't serve Retsina. I didn't know if I should applaud them for having good taste or curse them for cheating me of the opportunity to commune with Plato, Socrates and Maria Callas—if that opera singer ever drank wine.

The CO sipped his Greek beer and enthused how delicious it was. My husband tasted the beer and agreed that it was a great brew.

"But it's not Greek, it's Belgian" my spouse said. "Specifically, it's a Duvel Beer." The CO was adamant the beer was Greek and that he had discovered it like his ancestors had discovered America. He asked the café owner who shrugged and said it was Belgian—specifically, a Duvel beer. The CO was incredulous.

Greeks created democracy, dramatic plays and inspiring architecture but they didn't know how to make a beer this great.

"How could they?" my husband said, "When they add tree sap to wine?"

He did have a point.

After quaffing our delicious beers, the CO wished us a nice evening and excused himself. As the sound of his footsteps on the cobblestones faded, my cousin turned to me.

"You still want that glass of Retsina near the Parthenon?" I nodded. "Good because I know just the place to go."

And that he did.

20

A Simple Sauvignon Blanc

"You want anything from the store?" I said into the phone as I left work.

"Some Sauvignon Blanc," my husband said.

"What kind?"

"Just a simple Sauvignon Blanc."

Ahhh. Famous last words.

Sauvignon Blanc is a green grape traditionally grown in France's Loire Valley and Bordeaux regions. It likes a sunny, cool, maritime climate and thrives in France, California, South Africa, Chile and New Zealand. Its bud break occurs late and its fruit ripens early—so it's both a late bloomer and an early harvester. As a wine it's best served chilled and can be drunk all year long. It pairs well with meals of fish or sushi (Score!).

Okay, clearly this was the most amiable grape *ever*. Of course it would be easy to find "a simple" Sauvignon Blanc for the man in my life.

At the supermarket I perused the white wine section. There was a Sauvignon Blanc from Chile, which described itself as "fruity". There was a Sauvignon Blanc from New Zealand, which proclaimed it had hints of "citrus and passion fruit". There were several Sauvignon Blancs from California but they were labeled "Fumé Blanc" (French for "smoky white"). And there were a dozen bottles from France with mineral, florally notes yet all of them were called "Sancerres". Arghhh! Sauvignon Blancs weren't simple!

I dialed my husband.

"For your Sauvignon Blanc, do you want fruity, citrusy, or "smoky white"?"

"I'm in a meeting right now—"

"But—"

"Just pick one."

But which one? What would he be drinking this with? What would we be eating for dinner? OMG Dinner! I grabbed a cart and raced to the fish department. I asked the fishmonger for two filets of salmon. Wait! Salmon was heavy and this wine should have a lighter fish. Instead I got two filets of bass. I zoomed over to the carbs aisle where I chose between rice, quinoa and risotto by playing eeny, meany, miney, moe (quinoa won). Sprinting to the produce section I grabbed the freshest asparagus—

the ones as thin as art school pencils. Finally I looped back to the wine department and now armed with dinner, I'd know which Sauvignon Blanc to get.

Or not? Out of breath, patience and my last remaining dignity, I grabbed a bottle from Marlborough, New Zealand and bee-lined for the cash register. As I drove home dark clouds blotted out the evening sun. Who said Sauvignon Blanc was simple?! My husband? Well, I dare him to find a simple bottle to simply pair with simple food!

At home my husband sat down at the table for our white fish dinner with garlic quinoa, steamed asparagus and a bottle of Sauvignon Blanc. He poured himself a glass, swirled, sniffed and drank.

"Well?" I said biting my fingernail.

He shrugged. "It's just a simple Sauvignon Blanc—"

"But," my lips quivered. "That's what you wanted."

"—And it's simply perfect."

The dark clouds lifted, the angels sang. He liked it! Hooray! Sometimes wine selection and food pairing can be overwhelming. Before it reaches that point, I now remind myself why we're drinking wine: to enjoy one of life's pleasures. Simply.

21

Hosting a 20-Something Wine Party

"I wish I knew more about wine," my friend Roseanna said over drinks one night.

"Host a wine tasting party," I said.

"I'm 25. I don't have money for that."

"Can you afford to eat?"

"Yes."

"Then you can afford a wine tasting party."

Ahhh, being 20-Something. I remember those days of ramen noodle dinners, hand-me down furniture and buying clothes at thrift stores. I'm far from 20-Anything but I still shop at thrift stores because I relish the challenge of finding something great for a low price. Recently I found the most adorable shirt and pants by California designer Trina Turk in bright tropical colors and... but I digress.

Being 20-Something and not having a lot of cash does not prohibit you from hosting a swinging tasting party where you can learn about wine. Like thrifting, it's the challenge of doing something nice for a low price.

Here are 10 Tips to Host your own affordable 20-Something Wine Tasting Party:

1)   Every guest brings a bottle of wine. (*No one* is allowed to bring Trader Joe's Two Buck Chuck because *everyone* already knows what that wine tastes like.)

2)   Open all the bottles and set them in a central location on the table. Encourage guests to begin tasting the sparkling wines (aka Champagnes) first, then move on to the white wines, after which they can sample the red wines.

3)   Make a list of the wines drunk and, based on the other wines being sampled, rate them from 1-5 (with 5 being "the best"). Discuss with your friends what you smell, taste and like about the wine. Even if everyone likes the Pinot Noir and you don't, it's okay. Remember the goal is to discover what wines are available and which ones you like to drink.

4)   Provide a "dump bucket" for the wine. If a guest samples a wine but after tasting it does not like it they can pour it into this dump bucket.

Preferably use a deep dump bucket that is not clear glass. No one wants to see what's been dumped.

5)   Host your party on a weekend where you have time the day of to prepare for the party.

6)   Choose your music play list in advance. Some wine songs to include: "Spill the Wine" by the Isley Brothers, "Red, Red Wine" by UB40 and anything by Dean Martin.

7)   As the host, provide food to snack on. Do a colorful veggie tray with sliced cucumbers, red peppers, celery sticks, baby carrots and cherry tomatoes. Buy the vegetables whole so you can peel and slice them yourself, which is always cheaper— and healthier—than buying them pre-washed, pre-cut or pre-chewed.

8)   Make a cheese plate with mild varieties that will complement the wines, like Brie, Camembert, Gouda, or even a mild cheddar. (Cheese will be your biggest expense but a little goes a long way, which makes it worth it.)

9)   Decorate your cheese plate with thinly sliced apples, pears and/or red or green seedless table grapes. My favorite: Red Flame grapes.

10) Provide crackers to nibble on in between tasting the various wines. (Avoid salty crackers whose salt will mask the wine's flavors.)

But which wines to buy? Here's a list of 10 wines from our last tasting. I set a price limit: each bottle should cost $15 or less. Friends brought:

Sparkling Wines:
1) Cava: Freixnenet Cordon Negro from Spain (aka "The Spanish Champagne")

Whites:
2) Sauvignon Blanc: Sauvignon Republic from Marlborough, New Zealand
3) Chardonnay: Edna Valley Vineyard from California
4) Pinot Gris: A-Z from Oregon
5) Vinho Verde: Aveleda Fonte of Portugal

Reds:
6) Red wine blend: Epicurio Aglianico from Italy
7) Merlot (semi-sweet): Balatonboglári from Hungary
8) Grenache: Bitch (R Wines) from South Australia (Its name is fun if you don't take it personally.)
9) Malbec: 1 Antigal from Argentina
10) Cabernet Sauvignon: Ravenswood from California

10 tips to hosting a wine party + 10 wines that cost $15 and less = a terrific 20-Something Wine Tasting Party!

So whether you are 20-Something, 90-Something or somewhere in between, you can host your own affordable wine tasting party. I'm feeling so inspired I think I'll host one myself. And I know just the outfit I'll wear—the most adorable shirt and pants by California designer Trina Turk in bright tropical colors...

22

Ullage, Uvula, U Know

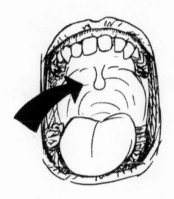

Ullage is one of those weird U words like umbrage, uvula and U know. But in wine it serves a purpose.

Ullage is the small space of air in the bottle between the top of the wine and the bottom of the cork. This air space is provided to allow for any expansion of the liquid during storage. As wine ages this space—the ullage—grows because the wine is evaporating slowly through the cork.

For centuries corks have been made from the wood of the—wait for it!—cork tree, which is a majestic evergreen oak native to the Mediterranean region. Fifty percent of the world's cork is grown in Portugal alone. Like grapes, cork is harvested, in this case from a mature tree, which means the tree is not chopped down but rather layers of the living tree's trunk bark are cut away to be fashioned into cork wine stoppers. One oak tree can be harvested a dozen or so times during its lifetime.

But with natural cork bottles, the ullage grows because precious wine—albeit just a little each year—is being lost. It's the 21st century, isn't there a better way to seal bottles?

Enter the lowly synthetic cork. With natural resources at a premium, some winemakers have embraced sealing bottles with the unlimited resource of plastic. Plastic corks prevent over-harvesting cork trees, keep the ullage from growing and can be used in kindergarten craft projects.

Once a bottle is opened, its wine is exposed to oxygen. At first this aeration will enhance the wine's flavor however, over time—hours or days—this oxygen turns the wine sour. Therefore if the bottle is not consumed at one sitting, it needs to be re-corked with its plastic wine stopper. But squeezing a plastic wine stopper back into a bottle is as easy as putting the Genie back into the bottle. It's the 21st century, isn't there a better way to reseal bottles?

Enter the lowly twist-off cap. Wine consumption continues to grow worldwide with China being the latest region to embrace the "nectar of the gods". While some wine lovers buy wine and save it for a rainy day sometime in the far-off future, most wine consumers—including China's billions—drink their wine within a week of buying it. In other words, they can't wait to suck it down. Taking a cue from soda manufacturers, the past 15 years have seen a rise in the number of vineyards opting to seal their bottles with twist-off caps.

Some of the first adopters of the twisties were white wine makers. Once opened white wine has a longer shelf life than red wine and if re-capped and stored in the refrigerator, can be drunk up to a week or so after opening. So why bother stuffing the natural cork or plastic cork back into the bottle? Why not be civilized and screw it back on?

It may be humble but a twist-off cap also means the ullage doesn't grow during storage, which means more wine for you, me and all those billions of Chinese wine fans.

It's the 21st century so there are plenty of opinions about this. There are some people who dislike the idea of wines topped with a metal twistie or a plastic cork, preferring their wines sealed with natural cork.

But the debate over which is better—cork vs. plastic cork vs. twist-off cap—is irrelevant. Winemakers choose the best sealant option for their wines and businesses. So it's not cork, synthetic cork *or* twistie, it's cork, synthetic cork *and* twistie.

And that's what really matters: getting the best bottle of wine U can, U know?

23

Vineyard... in the Backyard

"This year let's plant tomatoes in the backyard," I said at the home improvement store.

"Sure," my husband said putting a flat of tomatoes in the orange colored cart.

"And zucchini."

"Sure."

"And Cabernet Sauvignon grapes."

"... Excuse me?"

I am a do-it-myselfer and take pride in making my own things. I sew curtains, I knead pizza dough from scratch and unthinkably I make my wavy hair presentable on a daily basis. After years of apartment dwelling we bought our first house and my DIY zeal spread to the outdoors in the form of a vegetable garden, fig trees and an apricot orchard. I relish planting my own food, tending, harvesting and cooking it. One of the highlights of my backyard garden is plucking ripe tomatoes, still warm from the sun, and eating them in a fresh Caprese salad with home-grown basil. My vegetable garden was such a success last summer, why not expand it with winemaking grapes? Imagine: just three years from now I'll be floating in my own pool sipping a glass of my own wine, grown in my own backyard vineyard. That'd be the ultimate do-it-myselfer job!

"I don't think that's a good idea," my husband said scratching his head. "Growing your own wine grapes might make you dislike wine."

"Fat chance," I said ordering 67 books on home winemaking and quaffing a Malbec straight from the bottle. My husband looked at me as if I had gone off-the-grid bonkers.

Just to be sure I hadn't gone off-the-grid bonkers, I consulted the County's Cooperative Extension Office for the U.S. Department of Agriculture. If anyone knew the likely success of a backyard vineyard, it was those informed Aggies.

The Coop Extension Office raised some excellent points. First, I had to consider the sun and rain. Wine grapes needed about eight hours of sun a day and minimal water. Living in Los Angeles, I learned from singer Albert Hammond that "It never rains in Southern California"—except during February, El Nino years and when my Midwestern brother visits to play golf. So living in SoCal, my backyard vineyard idea was covered in the "*mucho* sun but little rain department".

According to the Aggies, I also had to consider the soil. Soil with too many nutrients was bad for grapes, soil with too much sand was bad for grapes, basically soil with too much of anything was bad for grapes. It seemed that growing a backyard vineyard followed the Ancient Greek Oracle at Delphi: "All things in moderation". It also followed the Golden State's tenet that everything grows in California, especially grapes, oranges and actors' egos. Living in SoCal, my backyard vineyard was covered in the "appropriate soil department".

Finally, the Aggies said I had to consider the acreage. How many acres of land would I be planting with grape vines: 200? 1,000? 5,000?

Whoa! I lived in the suburbs, I drove my own car, I cleaned my own house. Who did these Aggies think I was? A banker? A former president? A hip-hop singer? Well, I'm not. I belong to the 99% and just so happen to love wine.

"How much land do you have to convert to vineyard?" the Aggie asked.

"Ten square feet."

Silence.

"Okay. What's this?" the Aggie said poking my property map.

"My swimming pool." The Aggie suggested that I fill the pool with soil and plant vines in it. He wanted me to plant vines *In My Pool*.

I choked on my tongue. It had come to this: my backyard vineyard or my pool. What a Sophie's choice! I did not know how my backyard vineyard would grow in the space formerly known as my pool. But I did know that every day in the summer I enjoyed swimming in my beloved watering hole.

My husband was sort of right. I decided against planting a backyard vineyard not because it would make me dislike wine but because it would make me miss swimming. Besides there are so many excellent winemakers working today, how could I compete with them with my paltry 10 square feet? These days living anywhere in the world, I'm covered in the "plenty of excellent wines department".

So let's swim!

24

Wine Tasting Blind

"Darling, you're number 11!" Meredith said kissing my cheek, grabbing my wine bottle and pulling me into her kitchen where ten ladies swirled wineglasses.

"It's a red!" I hollered as my bottle, still wrapped in its brown paper bag, was passed from one manicured hand to another over the kitchen island's display of olives and pesto canapés. On the other side of the wood and black lacquer designer kitchen, Kari wrote "R11" with a black sharpie on the paper bag before sliding it in line with ten other brown-bagged bottles.

This month my all girl wine group was doing a blind tasting of California varietals. The rules for the night were simple: 1) Bring a bottle of what California grows best; 2) Taste each one; and without looking at the label 3) Guess the grape. Our group favors those who have a lot of experience with wine, so again, the winos among us had the advantage.

On a post-it note Kari published the variety types that were in play for the night. We had two whites—a Chardonnay and a Pinot Grigio. As well as nine reds—including three Cabernet Sauvignons, three Pinot Noirs, one Merlot, one Zinfandel and one Old World Syrah. The new girl to the group brought the French Syrah and since we're gals who care more about wine than rules, we popped the cork and added it to the mix.

With the others already sampling the reds, I moved quickly to the first white—W1—which had hints of straw and soil. I found W2 gave my tongue grassy notes, which transported my mind back to lazy summer afternoons when I was seven years-old lying straight as a log and rolling down the neighbor's hill over and over with the blades of grass brushing my giggling lips. Joining me in the laughing log roll was my sister and the neighbor girl. It was a delicious memory, as was the wine that brought it back to me.

"Darling, we're loving R5! Are you ready for it?" Meredith asked pointing the bottle's neck at me like a sawed-off shotgun. Her Australian accent was husky from years of wine drinking. Or was it cigarette smoking? I never could tell.

"I'm still catching up," I said pouring R3, which I found to be fruit forward with a dry finish although not as bone-dry as R4, which, after I swallowed a mouthful left my tongue more parched than it had been before I drank it. Finishes that pucker my mouth usually have more oaky tannins than my palate cares for. I like my wine in oak, not oak in my wine.

When I got to the bottle of R5 the ladies had ceased tasting it and were just plain guzzling it. Curious, I swirled some in my glass and breathed in; it had a fruity nose and its flavor was raspberry meets pepper, ending with a smooth finish. No wonder they hadn't moved on to the other seven bottles. It was like being on a Caribbean Island vacation and finding a secluded, sunny beach with waves. Why would you ever leave when you'd already found perfection?

Once we'd squeezed the last drops from R5 we sampled R6, R7, R8 and R9, which were like joining spring break's horny hordes at Fort Lauderdale after having vacationed at a private villa on St. Bart's.

"Darlings! We should have stopped with R5!" Meredith said wrinkling her nose and dumping out her glass of R9.

Just when despair was settling in, we were rescued by R10, a plum-flavored, fruit forward wine.

"It tastes like a popsicle stick," Kari said with a smile. "Sweet but with a dry ending."

We rounded off the evening with my little R11, which had hints of blackberry and pepper and ended with a full finish.

Finally, it was time for the unveiling. Kari pulled each bottle from its brown bag and from our list of pinots, merlots, etc., three winners stood out. Full disclosure: I was not able to guess all the grapes correctly. In fact, R6 utterly confused me: it was an old world grape grown in a new region in France which had picked up elements of the *terroir* I'd never tasted before. Lucky for me guessing correctly was not the point of the evening.

"Darlings," Meredith said as we formed a scrum around her kitchen island. "Tonight was a wake up call to forget what the label says and to trust our own taste buds. To rediscover what we— each of us—like." With that as the goal we definitely succeeded.

Unanimously our three favorite bottles of the night were a Rodney Strong Cabernet 2009.

"You can't go wrong with Rodney Strong!" Meredith croaked. We also liked my Layer Cake Cabernet Sauvignon 2009.

"Layer Cake! I want a piece of that," I sang to the cheering girls.

The biggest surprise of the night was the old vine Zinfandel from Seven Deadly Zins 2010. It's been almost a generation since the popular rise and fall of White Zin, so it's high time we remember the joy and flavor of America's own delicious Red Zinfandel. I'll be buying more of all these bottles.

While the gals rejoiced in reawakening their palates, I made a note of W2, the Chardonnay that brought back my childhood memory of grass rolls and laughter. No one else liked it but I didn't care.

Because that wine was all for me.

25

Xylem (of the Grape Plant)

While writing about wine from A-Z, friends have asked (with a devilish grin), "What will you write for X?"

Never fear! The world of wine is so vast it even includes one of those tricky X words: xylem.

The word "xylem" comes from the ancient Greek word "xylon", which means "wood or plank". Xylem is the woody, central part of the grape vine that transports water—the sap—from the roots to the rest of the plant. It also performs this function in other plants like roses, trees and poison ivy—all of which have xylems—but our focus is wine so we'll stick with the grape vines.

You can visualize the xylem as a one-way street that runs vertically from the top of the roots to the top of the plant. The xylem works in tandem with the phloem.

First, there is the normal process of photosynthesis, by which the plant converts the sunlight it absorbs into energy while turning carbon dioxide into oxygen for our breathing pleasure. This causes the plant to become dehydrated. If there is water in the soil, the plant's roots will absorb it, which causes pressure to accumulate in the roots forcing the sap containing the water to travel from the plant's roots through its xylem up to the rest of the plant for rehydration.

Conversely, the phloem is a one-way street that runs from the leaves to the rest of the plant. Every plant requires nutrients to grow. In grape plants the leaves produce the nutrients by converting the sunlight and carbon dioxide into sugars and amino acids, which are transported to the rest of the plant to be used immediately by the vine or stored for later use.

The xylem and phloem are vital parts of the grape vine's growth and if I say so myself, pretty darn incredible. So to all you X-word doubters out there: you can wipe off that devilish grin, pour yourself a glass of wine and toast to the xcellent, xtraordinary xylem already!

You're welcome!

26

Château d'Yquem

"Before you die, what's the one thing you want to do?" I asked over dinner.

"Go skydiving," my friend Pat said.

"Travel to Argentina's Pampas region," my husband said.

"Drink a bottle of 1811 Château d'Yquem Sauternes *Premier Cru Supérieur*," I said.

Silence.

If you're not a wine person it's hard to understand why I would long to drink a beverage that's over 200 years old. After all, wouldn't it be rotten by now? Oh ye of little faith! Let me explain.

Château d'Yquem is located in Bordeaux, France, one of the finest winemaking regions of the world. It is believed that when the Romans conquered southern France, they introduced winemaking to Bordeaux. Records indicate that the Château d'Yquem has been making wine since 1711, and perhaps as long ago as the late 1500s when it was deeded from the French King to a private citizen, Jacques de Sauvage. Just before the French Revolution, the Château and its vineyards came into the possession of the Lur-Saluces family, which to this day still holds a stake in the vineyard, albeit one shared with the luxury multi-conglomerate of Louis Vuitton-Moët Hennessy.

For centuries the Château d'Yquem has produced a world-famous white dessert wine called "Sauternes". This Sauternes is made of Sémillon and Sauvignon Blanc grapes and beginning with the 1855 vintage, Bordeaux wine connoisseurs have classified only this wine *Premier Cru Supérieur,* (French for "Superior First Growth"), which means it's special. How special? Oh ye doubters! Let me explain.

The d'Yquem Sauternes is made from grapes that have dried somewhat before harvesting and have been aided by the process of noble rot (in Greek: *Botrytis cinerea*). "Noble rot" is a genteel way of saying that while still on the vine, a fungus spontaneously grows on the surface of the grapes and consumes some of the fruit's water. This leaves a higher level of sugars and fruity acids in the grapes, which leads to the creation of a sweeter, more intense dessert wine.

It's bizarre to think that a fungus (usually a bad thing when growing between your toes) helps a wine become sweeter (usually a good thing like adding sugar to your tea). However, this isn't any old fungus, it's chemistry. The vineyards of the Château d'Yquem lie in a river valley that is covered in mist in the evening and warmed by the sun during the day. This cycle of mist, heat, mist, heat encourages the moldy fungus to grow on the grapes without harming them. Apparently the fungus has increased the quality and longevity of this wine.

In wine circles, there's a famous story about the world's premier wine critic tasting a Sauternes from Château d'Yquem. In 1996 Robert Parker sampled a bottle of the 1811 vintage—185 years after it was bottled—and found that its taste had improved over time, so much so that he gave it a perfect wine score of 100 points. On Mr. Parker's list of 100 wines that he awarded 100 points to, three vintages are from Château d'Yquem: the said 1811, the 1847 and the 2001.

To know a wine, is to love it. Thanks to wine geek sources like Mr. Parker, the Château's own Blog and my wine group, I have developed a passion for this wine, which longs to end in its consumption.

Across the table from me, I looked at my husband and Pat.

"So before you die, what do you say to tasting this wine?"

Silence.

113

"I'd still go skydiving," Pat said.

"I'd still travel to the Pampas region," my husband said.

Oh ye doubting Thomases! Well, good, that just means there will be more of that one bottle of Château d'Yquem Sauternes for me.

27

Zip-A-Dee-Doo-Dah, Zip-A-Dee-Ay, My Oh My What a Zinfandel Day

"You made it!" Monica said hugging my neck.

"I couldn't miss wine night!" I said stepping into her Spanish Colonial home.

"The others didn't feel the same way," Jill said sweeping her arm to the empty living room. "It's just the three of us tonight."

My wine group was of women, by women and for women. The only problem was we broads were busy with jobs, spouses and—except me— kids, so with a recurring event like our monthly wine club, it occasionally happened that some of the ladies could not make a particular wine night. But a wine night with just three women? Can you say "awkward"? Nervously my 30-something self looked from 20-something Jill to 40-something Monica. What could we possibly talk about? What kind of night would this be?

The night's theme was Zinfandel, a red grape of the *Vitis vinifera* family that grows well in California and is one of America's favorite wines. According to DNA, carbon dating and my own repeated personal testing, it's been determined that Zinfandel originated thousands of years ago in the Caucus region and is genetically similar to Italy's Primitivo grape found along the Dalmatian Coast. Zinfandel arrived in the USA in the mid-19th century and took to California's wine-growing climate like a woman to a two-for-one shoe sale.

Jill popped open her bottle of Zinfandel—in the glass it had a deep red color and tasted fruity, bursting with flavor in the mouth. Jill gushed how she'd bought this wine at a new wine store in her neighborhood. She talked about her job teaching first graders, which led to stories about DisneyLand, her three daughters and how all three girls wanted to grow up to be ballet dancers and astronauts—at the same time. The Zin that Jill brought was as lively as her conversation and as animated as Jill's

116

jubilant face. Although I was glad when she finally sipped her wine, it gave me time to catch my breath and sample the *vino*. And what a refreshing sip. It was like how a woman feels getting a pedicure: joy.

We poured my bottle of Zin and I cracked some jokes because that is what I do: I keep things light and engaging. We appreciated this vintage's red color and full jammy flavor. Verdict: it was just what I wanted. It was like how a woman feels getting a deep-tissue massage: pampered.

During the 1990s American winemakers produced an excess of red Zinfandel grapes so in an effort to find a new use for them, they created White Zinfandel. To make White Zin, vintners harvested the grapes and separated the red skins from the fruit, giving the wine the color of white wine. Then they added the skins back in—briefly— to give a rosé blush to this sweet wine. So White Zin is made of red grapes (read: weird) and is very sweet (read: weirder). This product was a hit when it came out and remains a popular wine for those with a sweet tooth—like my mother, my uncle and every wino on the planet.

None of us brought White Zin this night.

Monica uncorked her bottle of Zin. It was red like the two previous bottles but it was more intense and fuller. How could it be so different when it too was a red Zinfandel?

"This wine is made from Old Vine Zinfandel," Monica said. What makes an old vine? Usually it's a vine 20 years old or older. In California some Zinfandel vines are over 100 years old. In a fascinating twist, while many American vineyards in the 20th century lost their grape plants due to the phylloxera louse, the Zinfandel grape plants were not harmed by this pest. They continued to grow and prosper and today these vines make Old Vine Zinfandel wines.

Old vines produce a smaller quantity of grapes but the wine made from them tends to have fuller flavors and be more intense. While we sampled Monica's bottle she talked calmly about her job in finance, her spouse and their one young son.

"One child was enough for me," she said evenly. Monica's measured tones and stories masked a knowledge about the work-home life balance that challenges so many women. The wine she brought was as full and complex as she was. By the end of the evening, my appreciation for Old Vine Zin was like a woman's appreciation for diamonds: never-ending.

One night, three very different Zinfandels, three very different women and all of them were wonderful.

"Tonight, I'm glad it was just the three of us," Monica said.

I felt the same way.

28

Any Suggestions?

"Is this your first time to our wine bar?" the young bartender said sliding cocktail napkins toward my husband and me.

"Yes," I said as we claimed two barstools.

"You like wine?"

"Yes," I said.

"You need help ordering? I can give you some suggestions."

Pardon?

My spouse and I had left our sunny Los Angeles home to vacation for the first time in Washington State. Since it had rained every day of our trip it would also be our last time to Washington

State. We'd tried to see Mount Rainer but it was fogged in, we tried to see the Space Needle but it was hidden behind a cloud of umbrellas and now this impertinent kid bartender was trying to give me advice on wine?

Please. I'm in a wine group. I take wine vacations. I've been drinking it since the ancient Greeks. It was crystal clear to all the people who mattered—my husband and me—that if anyone should be offering wine advice, it was I to this youthful Millennial with the peach fuzz on his chin masquerading as a beard. He was barely 21 and he wanted to give me wine advice? Who does he think I am? A wine novice? A country hick? A damsel in wine distress?

I tossed the bartender a confident smile. "Thank you, but we don't need help ordering. And we don't need any suggestions."

"In that case, go for it," he said plunking a leather-bound book in front of us.

"Wine bars are handing out bibles now?" said the man I promised to love, honor and choose his wines for.

"It's their wine list gimmick," I said explaining how this establishment apparently was hoping to impress patrons if they presented their one-page wine list in a thick leather bible. It was like those Thai restaurants that put the check in a wooden box hoping you wouldn't dine and ditch or a shipwreck survivor who put a message in a bottle hoping for a miracle.

With the tome resting before us, I opened the cover and realized it wasn't a holy book stunt but a bound volume with plastic dividers containing full lists of wines, many wines, hundreds of wines. I flipped through the pages and pages of wine names—this was a wine treasury, a wine diamond mine, the Fort Knox of wines. Bingo!

"See anything good?" my husband asked spinning his cocktail napkin on the bar's polished concrete surface. I shook my head. "You don't like anything?" he said with surprise.

"I don't recognize anything." Over the years I'd tasted and loved scores of wines from California to Chile, from Napa to Naples. But none of the hundreds of names on the wine list rang a bell with me.

"Let's ask the bartender for help," he said.

"Can I get you something from the wine list?" the bartender said sidling up to us.

"Yes," said my husband. "What do you suggest—"

"No," I said plastering a smile on my face to mask the dismay in my voice. "We just need more time." Placating a thirsty spouse, battling a pushy bartender and fighting an unknown wine list were raising the stakes on the evening. Nevertheless the challenge of finding a good wine on my own helped me rally. I couldn't let the Bartender think I didn't know wine. I'd show him! Ha!

The world is divided into three types of people: 1) People who read something once and photographically remember it forever; 2) People who see something once and remember it visually for a long time; 3) People who can't remember anyth— Uh, what was I saying? Ever since I was a kid, I've been a visual learner: I need to see it to remember it. Of course! If I could just see the labels I'd recognize a wine that I already knew, which we could order.

The wine bar was in a converted warehouse that rose three stories high. In the center of the room stood the establishment's *pièce de résistance*—a massive tower of wine bottles rising to the ceiling, bound and accessed by a circular stairway. I watched waiters zip up the stairs and come down carrying bottles to serve customers. With their permission, the man I promised to love, honor and keep things interesting for held our seats at the bar while I went exploring.

From a distance it looked like London's White Tower that imprisoned the young nephews of England's Richard the III before they were murdered by their dear uncle. But up close, the structure was a huge wine rack holding over 4,500 bottles. The mother lode!

I entered the second floor room of the tower and scanned the labels, no, nothing, nope. I raced up and down the stairs visually looking at every bottle only to realize all the labels were from Washington State and therefore complete unknowns to me. I was in *Vitis vinifera incognita*.

I returned to the bar to find my spouse folding his cocktail napkin into a paper plane.

"I'm ready to drink. Did you find something to order?" Dejected, I shook my head.

"Can I get you some wine from the tower?" the bartender said appearing before us like a mirage in a western desert.

"Yes," said my husband. "What do you sugges—"

"No!" I said locking my eyes with the bartender.

"Can I offer some wine suggestions?"

I shook my head. "We're still deciding."

"But I'm thirsty—" my husband sniffed. The baby-faced bartender and I exchanged long looks. He looked sweet but he was crafty. I stood firm in my cowboy boots. A harmonica sounded. If there had been any tumbleweeds in Seattle they would have blown across our path.

"We need more time," I said in an even tone. The bartender nodded and sauntered to the other side of the bar. Just seeing his fresh-faced cheeks up close gave me strength. I didn't need him or his suggestions, I could find a wine for the man I promised to love, honor and not embarrass. It was imperative I find a wine from this place that would quench my husband's thirst and blow this bartender's high school gym socks off.

"I want to drink something. Anything," my husband said.

"You will, we will—"

"When?"

"I have a plan."

My plan was simple: I'd just ask another customer what he was drinking and thereby get a great wine name to satisfy my husband and impress this bartender. Ha! I turned to the guy next to me and smiled.

"It looks like you have good taste.

"You're right."

"What are you drinking?"

"A lite beer."

"In a wine bar?" The guy shrugged. My plan had failed. My husband stopped himself from screaming only by stuffing a cocktail napkin in his own mouth. Things were grim. Looking my spouse in the eye I saw the desperation. Not the regular desperation—believe me, I'd seen it often enough to visually remember it—but a new level of desperation, one that doctors called "Everest Level". Right after reaching Everest Level things went downhill fast. I had to act. I had to do something to save my pride and nourish the man I'd promised to love, honor and stop frustrating.

My head drooped to the bar's gleaming surface. I pushed my pride off Everest's mountaintop and gazed up at the bartender. I embraced my painful reality: I was a damsel in wine distress.

"Help," I whimpered.

The bartender leaped to work flipping back and forth among the wine list's countless pages pointing out local wines while jabbering on about the Evergreen State's American Viticultural Areas (AVAs) like the Rattlesnake Hills, the Yakima

Valley, the Wahluke Slope and the Walla Walla. It was wonderful. The youthful bartender was thrilled to share his vast knowledge about these Northwest wines, I relished learning something new and my husband was thankful that good wine was in his very near future.

The wines came, we sniffed, we drank, we were conquered by Washington wines. Despite the rain, I swore to return to Washington State because their bartenders were pushy and the wines were that good. I still think it's wrong for a boy-man whose voice hasn't changed yet to give me advice about wines, but now I never pass up the opportunity to take wine suggestions.

So I'll share my own suggestions with you: Drink wine and enjoy it!

ACKNOWLEDGEMENTS

I'd like to thank Sharmyn McGraw for feedback, Gayle Carline and Sheri Fink for answering questions and my fabulous Blog readers for reading. I'd also like to thank Chris Grun for help and my Wine Group for being terrific ladies with some amazing noses. Finally, I'd like to give a special thanks to my husband for being so tolerant of all the research that went into this book, for his perfectionism, his artistic eye for detail, for creating the book's cover and illustrations, and in general, for him being such a wonderful guy.

ABOUT THE AUTHOR

Alicia Bien is a comedy writer, performer and wine lover. She studied at Second City-Hollywood and the Upright Citizens Brigade and is Head Writer for the sketch show "Top Story! Weekly" at iO West. She lives in Los Angeles with her husband and adopted cat. Visit the author online at her Blog newhousegirl.blogspot.com and follow her at Twitter@aliciabien.

8021926R00083

Made in the USA
San Bernardino, CA
26 January 2014